INTIMATE EXPANSES

INTIMATE EXPANSES

XXV Scottish Poems
1978–2002

Edited by Ken Cockburn and Robyn Marsack

CARCANET

SCOTTISH POETRY LIBRARY

By leaves we live

First published in 2004 by

The Scottish Poetry Library
5 Crichton's Close
Canongate
Edinburgh
EH8 8DT

and

Carcanet Press Limited
Alliance House
Cross Street
Manchester
M2 7AQ

ISBN 1 85754 795 0

The publishers acknowledge support from the Scottish Arts Council towards the publication of this title.

Designed and typeset in Shaker by Barrie Tullett

Printed and bound by
The Cromwell Press, Trowbridge, Wiltshire

Scottish
Arts Council
LOTTERY FUNDED

Contents

Editorial Note

This selection was made on the principle of one poem per year. The poem in question may have appeared in a magazine or a collection that year. Publication details appear within the biographies.

We are grateful to the poets, editors and academics who answered our request to suggest poems for inclusion. Certain poems, which were chosen by several respondents to our request, formed a backbone to our selection; while other poems, suggested by a single respondent and which otherwise we may have overlooked, were drawn to our attention.

This anthology is the first in a series, all of which come under the XXV heading. This selection of Scottish poems will be translated into a number of European languages, and published in several European editions; in return, we will receive several representative selections of 25 poems, all covering the period 1978–2002, which Scottish poets and translators will make English or Scots versions of. The first partnerships are with Hungary and Finland, with others to follow.

The resources of the Scottish Poetry Library were essential to our work, in particular the Scottish Poetry Index, which lists poems published in magazines. We are delighted to be publishing this book in 2004, the year which marks the Library's twentieth anniversary.

Ken Cockburn
Robyn Marsack

Intimate Expanses:
XXV Scottish Poems, 1978–2002

Over this quarter century, one of the recurring questions people in Scotland have asked themselves is: what does it mean to be Scottish? The way poets have responded to, or avoided, this question, is one way of attempting an overview of the period.

The question is all the more pressing in that there is no obvious answer. Scotland has not been independent since political union with England in 1707, and linguistically it was split between the traditionally Gaelic-speaking minority in the highlands and islands, and the Scots-speaking majority in the lowlands; although in both areas English has increasingly become the dominant language. It maintained a kind of civic independence, with its own distinctive education and legal systems, and its own church separate from the established (i.e. state-governed) Church of England.

In the 19th century emigration, often forced, from the highlands marginalised Gaelic communities, and immigration from Ireland led to class and religious tensions in the industrial central belt. Nonetheless, the expansion of the British Empire led to industrial growth and prosperity, and there was little demand for 'Home Rule' compared with the situation in Ireland. A Scottish nationalist movement was formed in the 1920s, following the establishment of many smaller nations at the end of the First World War; parallel with this, socialist and communist movements developed, less concerned with Scotland as a nation in its own right than with the emancipation of the working classes throughout the United Kingdom.

The most influential Scottish poet from the 1920s to the 1970s was Hugh MacDiarmid (1892–1978). His early collections of short lyrics, and the long poem *A Drunk Man Looks at the Thistle* (1926) established Modernism in Scotland, by incorporating versions of work by contemporary European poets, and the collaging of Scots vocabulary from different eras, regions and registers to create what he called 'synthetic Scots'. Politically, MacDiarmid was a maverick who managed to be expelled from both the Nationalist and Communist Parties. After suffering poverty and neglect in the 1930s and 1940s, by the 1950s he was becoming increasingly recognised as a Great Poet. During the last two decades of his life, in his public persona at least, he became a patriarchal, authoritarian figure, whom one was either resolutely for or against.

As this anthology begins in the year of MacDiarmid's death, it seems appropriate to open not with a poem by the old poet, but with a poem about the death of the father. Alastair Reid's touching, personal poem concludes not with a ending but a beginning, of 'that hesistant conversation / which will go on and on'. Indirectly all the writers of this quarter century are linked to MacDiarmid, in the sense that he provided the model of a poet questioning issues of identity, politics, culture, metaphysics and language within this shared geography which we call Scotland.

The speaking, intimate voice of Reid's poem is not untypical here: language is something to be used in a concrete manner, a form of address to the other, whether a specific 'character' as here, or the reader more generally. Douglas Dunn's 'Empires' is also a poem about death, but this time of of a society rather than an individual. Its jerky rhythms, and its us/them divide, mark both the end of Empire, and the beginning of a paradoxical triumphalism. 1979 saw the end of socialism in the UK, and the election to power of Margaret Thatcher, ushering in 18 years of Conservative government. Thatcher oversaw both the rundown of heavy industries with subsequent high unemployment levels, and a flag-waving military success against Argentina in the 1982 war over the Falkland Islands. In Scotland the Conservative Party never had a majority of Scottish MPs; in fact their numbers dwindled steadily from election to election, leading to an increasing sense of government imposed rather than chosen. During this period, the arts in general, and literature in particular, came to stand for a de facto cultural independence, in the absence of actual political independence.

Edwin Morgan's *Sonnets from Scotland* present episodes from Scottish history, from prehistoric times through recorded history and the contemporary into the future. The sequence attempts an integrated vision of Scotland through time, not fixing it as something 'authentic' to be protected against dilution, corruption or debasement, but actively welcoming its transformations: place as journey. 'The Coin' was resonant in the early 1980s, with its unearthing of a realised Scottish republic.

Morgan's earlier poems had redefined literary views of Glasgow, and inspired a generation of younger writers living in the city, including Tom Leonard, Liz Lochhead and Alan Spence. Compared to Edinburgh, Glasgow had been little explored in literature, and all these writers took this as an opportunity. Spence mixed myth and eastern religion with realistic depictions of life in the city; Lochhead brought a female perspective to a traditionally male, even macho, culture; and Leonard used the rhythms and vocabulary of contemporary Glaswegian speech to examine the way language both hides and reveals subtleties of thought. Leonard's acknowledged model for his non-standard English was not the Scots tradition, but the American poet William Carlos Williams, who had attempted to create a poetry based on actual American speech as opposed to the conventions of literary written English.

Lochhead was the first of a number of women poets who came to prominence in the 1980s and 1990s. Carol Ann Duffy was born and spent her early childhood in Glasgow, before moving with her family to the English midlands. She has become a very popular poet, sensitive to the linguistic inanities which accompanied the boom-bust economic cycles of the Thatcher years, and of women's lives both contemporary and historical. 'Warming her Pearls' offers a note of eroticism otherwise lacking in Scottish poetry through this period. Kathleen Jamie has remained in Scotland, and her work increasingly integrates Scots vocabulary and syntax into what remain recognisably poems in English. Her work has been concerned with redefining Scotland, with its tensions of urban and rural, archaic and post-modern, repressive and liberating, male and female. Gerrie Fellows' poem is from a sequence looking back at Scottish emigration to New Zealand, her own birthplace, and again highlights the question of Scottish identity. This anthology includes work by those 'Scottish by formation', that is born in Scotland or of Scottish parentage (but perhaps living abroad); or resident in Scotland (whatever one's background). Such a definition of Scottishness has become more widespread over the past decade or so.

Jamie and Duffy were both included in the 1994 'New Generation' promotion; twenty younger poets were selected and heavily promoted, with poetry presented as 'the new rock 'n' roll'. Scotland was over-represented: of the twenty, seven were 'Scottish by formation'. They included Robert Crawford, Don Paterson, John Burnside and W.N. Herbert; with Jamie, they marked a shift away from Glasgow as the literary hub of Scotland to Tayside – specifically Dundee and the small university town of St Andrews. All are published by English presses, and have a high profile throughout the UK, and abroad. As had previously happened with Glasgow, the Dundee-born poets Paterson and Herbert took the city's lack of literary heritage as an opportunity, a blank canvas, though their subject matter ranges widely beyond the city itself. 'Nil Nil' is the title poem of Paterson's striking debut collection of 1993. Like Jamie he uses Scots within English; thinking and living mainly in English, but with a resevoir of Scots words from childhood and contemporary usage. Herbert, like Robert Crawford with whom he collaborated in the years before and after 1990, draws directly on MacDiarmid's notion of 'synthetic Scots', but expands it to take in words from all sorts of archaic and contemporary dialects or jargons. Herbert writes extended, fantastical, often humorous poems, his unlimited lexis opening up the strangest perspectives, while in 'Scotland' Crawford typically juxtaposes old and new – placenames and technology – to create a deliberately startling conjunction of vocabularies, rather than aiming for a smoothness or evenness of language. John Burnside's phrase, 'our difficult and unrelenting love', echoes Alastair Reid's sentiments, and can be read as an attitude to Scotland as a whole, rather than a particular individual or tradition.

Following the achievements of Sorley MacLean in the 1930s and 1940s, Gaelic had been reinvigorated as a medium for modern poetry. MacLean remained an inspirational presence until his death in 1996. Meg Bateman represents a new type of Gaelic poet, one born not in the 'heartland' of the highlands and islands but in Edinburgh, who learned Gaelic as a second language. She has brought new perspectives to the language in terms of form and subject matter, particularly an intimate sense of love and loss, at some remove from the more formal love poetry of earlier generations. Kevin MacNeil, while a native speaker, has broadened Gaelic literature's horizons by incorporating aspects of oriental throught and religion. Aonghas Macneacail, another native speaker, writes of the birth of his own first child, but the poem also conveys the sense that Gaelic has a future as well as a past.

Iain Crichton Smith wrote prose and poetry both in Gaelic and English. His knowledge of the Gaelic tradition gives his English-language poetry a resource few other poets writing in Scots or English have been able to draw on (unlike in Ireland, where most of the main English-language poets have a knowledge of Irish Gaelic language and literature). Smith uses the strict presbyterianism of the Lewis community in which he grew up as a touchstone throughout his work, rejecting what he sees as its repressive confines, but constantly testing his existential spontaneous vision of the world against those rigours. Norman MacCaig, the oldest poet included here, and for many years a close friend of MacDiarmid, lived in Edinburgh and wrote in English, but the recurrent landscapes in his work are those of the north-west highlands, where he spent his summers. As a young poet in the 1940s, he was linked with the 'Apocalypse' group, but he gradually came reject its ecstatic complexity in favour of simpler utterances, while still attempting to capture the connectedness, the multiple levels, of reality. Gael Turnbull also draws from the Gaelic tradition, looking simultaneously backwards and forwards. As he discovers and admires archaic words for deeply specialist concepts, he presents equivalent contemporary concepts for which as yet no words exist, thus implictly criticising the limitations of contemporary English, world language or not.

With the election of a Labour government in 1997, and its immediate decision to enact devolution for Scotland, the political mood changed from one of opposition and challenge to celebration and acceptance, and a refocusing – both inwards on the personal, and outwards to the wider world. The last few poems in the book reflect this increased self-confidence, from Iain Bamforth's vast list of things, large and small, to celebrate the parliament's opening, to Andrew Greig's paean to his adopted home of Orkney. The book ends with a poem by Richard Price to his daughter, who suffers from Angelman Syndrome and finds it hard to fall asleep. At one level a gentle lullaby, the poem is also an expression of frustration at the child's inability to 'switch off', and can stand for the 24/7 information-rich society where there is, in Edwin Morgan's phrase, 'nothing not giving messages'. The poet's task is becoming less the providing of information and the shaping of myths or lyrical moments for the reader, and more offering a space for contemplation, a space where the constant white noise can be switched off and the mind contemplate itself and the world, unmediated. That has always been a dynamic contradiction of art, to use language to make a silence.

Finally, there are three poems which are harder to categorise, all written by poets with very individual voices who worked or work outside the literary mainstream. Robin Fulton left Scotland in the 1970s to live in Norway, and has since written about his birthplace with a certain distance and detatchment. George Campbell Hay writes of a tradition in decline, though the poem itself is full of energy. Seán Rafferty's early work was admired by Sorley MacLean, but was only 'rediscovered' towards the end of his life.

They offer a reminder that poetry may fit into a neat narrative pattern in hindsight, but is made by individuals at a particular moment in a particular set of circumstances. While patterns of influence and connectedness exist through time, one must also acknowledge the independence of the individual poem, and the one-to-one relationship that exists between poems and readers, who bring their own moment and circumstance to their reading. One of the reasons for compiling this anthology is to transmit poems from here to there, and see what happens. Reader, in whichever language you read these poems, the rest is up to you.

Ken Cockburn
July 2004

THE POEMS

My Father, Dying

At summer's succulent end,
the house is green-stained.
I reach for my father's hand

and study his ancient nails.
Feeble-bodied, yet at intervals
a sweetness appears and prevails.

The heavy-scented night
seems to get at his throat.
It is as if the dark coughed.

In the other rooms of the house,
the furniture stands mumchance.
Age has graved his face.

Cradling his wagged-out chin,
I shave him, feeling bone
stretching the waxed skin.

By his bed, the newspaper lies furled.
He has grown too old
to unfold the world,

which has dwindled to the size of a sheet.
His room has a stillness to it.
I do not call it waiting, but I wait,

anxious in the dark, to see if
the butterfly of his breath
has fluttered clear of death.

There is so much might be said,
dear old man, before I find you dead;
but we have become too separate

now in human time
to unravel all the interim
as your memory goes numb.

But there is no need for you to tell —
no words, no wise counsel,
no talk of dying well.

We have become mostly hands
and voices in your understanding.
The whole household is pending.

I am not ready
to be without your frail and wasted body,
your miscellaneous mind-way,

the faltering vein of your life.
Each evening, I am loth
to leave you to your death.

Nor will I dwell on
the endless, cumulative question
I ask, being your son.

But on any one
of these nights soon,
for you, the dark will not crack with dawn,

and then I will begin
with you that hesitant conversation
going on and on and on.

Alastair Reid | 1978

Empires

All the dead Imperia ... They have gone
Taking their atlases and grand pianos.
They could not leave geography alone.
They conquered with the thistle and the rose.
To our forefathers it was right to raise
Their pretty flag at every foreign dawn
Then lower it at sunset in a haze
Of bugle-brass. They interfered with place,
Time, people, lives, and so to bed. They died
When it died. It had died before. It died
Before they did. They did not know it. Race,
Power, Trade, Fleet, a hundred regiments,
Postponed that final reckoning with pride,
Which was expensive. Counting up the cost
We plunder morals from the power they lost.
They ruined us. They conquered continents.
We filled their uniforms. We cruised the seas.
We worked their mines and made their histories.
You work, we rule, they said. We worked; they ruled.
They fooled the tenements. All men were fooled.
It still persists. It will be so, always.
Listen. An out-of-work apprentice plays
God Save the Queen on an Edwardian flute.
He is, but does not know it, destitute.

right inuff

right inuff
ma language is disgraceful

ma maw tellt mi
ma teacher tellt mi
thi doactir tellt mi
thi priest tellt mi

ma boss tellt mi
ma landlady in carrington street tellt mi
thi lassie ah tried tay get aff way in 1969 tellt mi
sum wee smout thit thoat ah hudny read chomsky tellt mi
a calvinistic communist thit thoat ah wuz revisionist tellt mi

po-faced literati grimly kerryin thi burden a thi past tellt mi
po-faced literati grimly kerryin thi burden a thi future tellt mi
ma wife tellt mi jist-tay-get-inty-this-poem tellt mi
ma wainz came hame fray school an tellt mi
jist aboot ivry book ah oapnd tellt mi
even thi introduction tay thi Scottish National Dictionary tellt mi

ach well
all livin language is sacred
fuck thi lohta thim

Tom Leonard | 1980

My Rival's House

is peopled with many surfaces.
Ormolu and gilt, slipper satin,
lush velvet couches,
cushions so stiff you can't sink in.
Tables polished clear enough to see distortions in.

We take our shoes off at her door,
shuffle stocking-soled, tiptoe — the parquet floor
is beautiful and its surface must
be protected. Dust
cover, drawn shade,
won't let the surface colour fade.

Silver sugar-tongs and silver salver
my rival serves us tea.
She glosses over him and me.
I am all edges, a surface, a shell
and yet my rival thinks she means me well.
But what squirms beneath her surface I can tell.
Soon, my rival
capped tooth, polished nail
will fight, fight foul for her survival.
Deferential, daughterly, I sip
and thank her nicely for each bitter cup.

And I have much to thank her for.
This son she bore —
first blood to her —
never, never can escape scot free
the sour potluck of family.
And oh how close
this family that furnishes my rival's place.

Lady of the house.
Queen bee.

She is far more unconscious,
far more dangerous than me.
Listen, I was always my own worst enemy.
She has taken even this from me.

She dishes up her dreams for breakfast.
Dinner, and her salt tears pepper our soup.
She won't
give up.

Liz Lochhead | 1981

Museums and Journeys

An exhibition: a hundred years of Edinburgh life.
Coming out I move as heavily as a diver
on the ocean floor: one step, one breath
against the weight of the invisible dead. So many
yet the air is clear. And they've no time for me,
their view of the future blocked by giant headlines.

A journey: one I didn't want to take but took
shutting my eyes – a child again hoping the needle
wouldn't hurt. Lakes and forests, lakes and forests
pass with the weightless ease of delirium. So many.
My view of the past stays clear but hard to read
like a radio-map of a secret corner in the night sky.

Museums and journeys. We meet as strangers do
at the end of long ellipses over continents.
We exchange histories. Our view of the present is clear
but the landscapes go on sliding past. So many
memories, I try to say 'One at a time!'
They keep piling up like urgent unanswered letters.

The Coin

We brushed the dirt off, held it to the light.
The obverse showed us *Scotland*, and the head
of a red deer; the antler-glint had fled
but the fine cut could still be felt. All right:
we turned it over, read easily *One Pound*,
but then the shock of Latin, like a gloss,
Respublica Scotorum, sent across
such ages as we guessed but never found
at the worn edge where once the date had been
and where as many fingers had gripped hard
as hopes their silent race had lost or gained.
The marshy scurf crept up to our machine,
sucked at our boots. Yet nothing seemed ill-starred.
And least of all the realm the coin contained.

Edwin Morgan | 1983

'Iolaire'

On New Year's Eve 1918 a ship called the *Iolaire* left Kyle of Lochalsh to bring three hundred men home to Lewis after the war was over. On New Year's morning 1919 the ship went on the rocks as a result of a navigational error at the Beasts of Holm, a short distance from Stornoway, the main town on the island. About two hundred sailors were drowned. In the following poem I imagine an elder of the church speaking as he is confronted with this mind-breaking event.

The green washed over them. I saw them when
the New Year brought them home. It was a day
that orbed the horizon with an enigma.
It seemed that there were masts. It seemed that men
buzzed in the water round them. It seemed that fire
shone in the water which was thin and white
unravelling towards the shore. It seemed that I
touched my fixed hat which seemed to float and then
the sun illumined fish with naval caps,
names of the vanished ships. In sloppy waves,
in the fat of water, they came floating home
bruising against their island. It is true,
a minor error can inflict this death.
That star is not responsible. It shone
over the puffy blouse, the flapping blue
trousers, the black boots. The seagull swam
bonded to the water. Why not man?
The lights were lit last night, the tables creaked
with hoarded food. They willed the ship to port
in the New Year which would erase the old,
its errant voices, its unpractised tones.
Have we done ill, I ask, my fixed body
a simulacrum of the transient waste,
for everything was mobile, planks that swayed,
the keeling ship exploding and the splayed
cold insect bodies. I have seen your church
solid. This is not. The water pours
into the parting timbers where I ache

above the globular eyes. The slack heads turn
ringing the horizon without sound,
with mortal bells, a strange exuberant flower
unknown to our dry churchyards. I look up.
The sky begins to brighten as before,
remorseless amber, and the bruised blue grows
at the erupting edges. I have known you, God,
not as the playful one but as the black
thunderer from hills. I kneel
and touch this dumb blond head. My hand is scorched.
Its human quality confuses me.
I have not felt such hair so dear before
nor seen such real eyes. I kneel from you.
This water soaks me. I am running with
its tart sharp joy. I am floating here
in my black uniform. I am embraced
by these green ignorant waters. I am calm.

By the graveyard, Luskentyre

From behind the wall death sends out messages
That all mean the same, that are easy to understand.

But who can interpret the blue-green waves
That never stop talking, shouting, wheedling?

Messages everywhere. Scholars, I plead with you,
Where are your dictionaries of the wind, the grasses?

Four larks are singing in a showering sprinkle
Their bright testaments: in a foreign language.

And always the beach is oghamed and cuneiformed
By knot and dunlin and country-dancing sandpipers.

—There's Donnie's lugsail. He's off to the lobsters.
The mast tilts to the north, the boat sails west.

A dictionary of him? —Can you imagine it? —
A volume thick as the height of the Clisham,

A volume big as the whole of Harris,
A volume beyond the wit of scholars.

Five Haiku

the puppy
ferociously challenging
a daffodil

the moon moves with us
as we walk,
drifts from tree to tree

mouse-tracks
across the frozen lard
in the frying pan

remembering
my father's death –
cold november rain

the snowman
calmly awaiting
the thaw

Alan Spence | 1986

Warming Her Pearls

for Judith Radstone

Next to my own skin, her pearls. My mistress
bids me wear them, warm them, until evening
when I'll brush her hair. At six, I place them
round her cool, white throat. All day I think of her,

resting in the Yellow Room, contemplating silk
or taffeta, which gown tonight? She fans herself
whilst I work willingly, my slow heat entering
each pearl. Slack on my neck, her rope.

She's beautiful. I dream about her
in my attic bed; picture her dancing
with tall men, puzzled by my faint, persistent scent
beneath her French perfume, her milky stones.

I dust her shoulders with a rabbit's foot,
watch the soft blush seep through her skin
like an indolent sigh. In her looking-glass
my red lips part as though I want to speak.

Full moon. Her carriage brings her home. I see
her every movement in my head . . . Undressing,
taking off her jewels, her slim hand reaching
for the case, slipping naked into bed, the way

she always does ... And I lie here awake,
knowing the pearls are cooling even now
in the room where my mistress sleeps. All night
I feel their absence and I burn.

from Seeker, Reaper

She's a solan, she's a tramper, she's a sea-shaker,
she's a hawk, she's a hammer, she's a big-sea-breaker,
she's a falcon, she's a kestrel, she's a wide-night-seeker,
she's a river, she's a render, she's a foam-spray-waker.
She's a stieve sea-strider, she's a storm-course-keeper,
she's a tide-scour-bucker, she's a quick-light-leaper,
she's a stem-teerer, keel-teerer, seeker, finder, reaper.
She's *Cast off! Anchor up!* deid anchor-weary,
she's a chain-snubber, moorin'-strainer, restless herbour peerie.
She's a skyline-raiser, skyline-sinker, hulldown horizon-crosser,
she's foreland, foreland, on and on, a high-heid-tosser.
She's a glint, she's a glimmer, she's a glimpse, she's a fleeter,
she's an overhauler, leave-astern, a hale-fleet-beater;
she's a kyle-coulter, knot-reeler, thrang-speed-spinner,
her mood is moulded on her and the mind that made her's in her.
She's a wake-plough, foam-plough, spray-hammer, roarer,
she's a wind-anvil, crest-batterer, deep-trough-soarer,
she's a dance-step-turner, she's a broad-wake-scorer,
She's a sound-threider, bight stringer, her hert runs oot afore her.
When the big long seas come on lik walls, cold-white-heided,
she doesna flinch a point for them. Straight her wake is threided.

George Campbell Hay | 1988

Aotromachd

B' e d' aotromachd a rinn mo thàladh,
aotromachd do chainnte 's do ghàire,
aotromachd do lethchinn nam làmhan,
d' aotromachd lurach ùr mhàlda;
agus 's e aotromachd do phòige
tha a' cur trasg air mo bheòil-sa,
is 's e aotromachd do ghlaic mum chuairt-sa
a leigeas seachad leis an t-sruth mi.

Lightness

It was your lightness that drew me,
the lightness of your talk and your laughter,
the lightness of your cheek in my hands,
your sweet gentle modest lightness;
and it is the lightness of your kiss
that is starving my mouth,
and the lightness of your embrace
that will let me go adrift.

Scotland

Semiconductor country, land crammed with intimate expanses,
Your cities are superlattices, heterojunctive
Graphed from the air, your cropmarked farmlands
Are epitaxies of tweed.

All night motorways carry your signal, swept
To East Kilbride or Dunfermline. A brightness off low headlands
Beams-in the dawn to Fife's interstices,
Optoelectronics of hay.

Micro-nation. So small you cannot be forgotten,
Bible inscribed on a ricegrain, hi-tech's key
Locked into the earth, your televised Glasgows
Are broadcast in Rio. Among circuitboard crowsteps

To be miniaturised is not small-minded.
To love you needs more details than the Book of Kells -
Your harbours, your photography, your democratic intellect
Still boundless, chip of a nation.

Robert Crawford | 1990

little mouth

little mouth,
tell me
in your new language
how your mother
filled with you –
remember that?

little mouth,
sing to me
in your new language
the young songs
that started time

little mouth,
make for me
the shape of your feeding

little mouth,
what's the sport,
give me the colour
of your day

hold, hold
little mouth,
too fast for me,
your syllables
flood over me
in torrents of
white lightning,
stabbing the hard flesh
of my patience

little mouth
little mouth,
would you
          eat me?

beul beag

a bheòil bhig,
an inns' thu dhomh
nad chànan ùr
mar a lìon
do mhàthair leat –
eil cuimhn' agad

a bheòil bhig,
an seinn thu dhomh
nad chànan ùr
na h-òrain òg
a thòisich tìm

a bheòil bhig,
an dèan thu cruth
do bhiathaidh dhomh

a bheòil bhig,
dé 'n cleas,
an toir thu tuar
do latha dhomh

seas, seas
a bheòil bhig,
cha tuig mi thu,
tha eas do lidean
taomadh orm
mar dhealain geal
a' sàthadh feòil chruaidh
m'fhoighidinn

a bheòil bhig
a bheòil bhig,
an ith thu mi?

Aonghas Macneacail | 1991

little mouth,
you're not the first
to say *i am*

little mouth,
purse of noises
still as a rose,
now harbour of sleep

little mouth,
when you return from
the dumb glen
tell those
who haven't heard
your new language
that you don't like pain

a bheòil bhig,
cha tus' an aon
tha gairm do bhith

a bheòil bhig,
sporain nam fuaim
nad ròs réidh
's tu cala 'n t-suain

a bheòil bhig,
nuair a thilleas tu
à gleann nam balbh
an inns' thu dhaibh
nach cual thu fòs
nad chànan ùr
nach toigh leat cràdh

Aonghas Macneacail | 1991

Peacocks

I would be Adam
leafless in the garden
with all my ribs about me
one day more.
For one more day
the Voice be off the air:
a Heavenly silence
in which I find my feet
and flex my fingers
to grasp the Situation.

I doan like it.

To be creation's clown
a six-day wonder
a ten-toed bi-ped
with this bag of pebbles
that wobble when I walk.

He should have held his breath.
Five days was plenty.
Earth, sea, beasts, fowl; then feet up.

Make feathers fly and finish.

Peacocks.
Full stop.

Peacocks was really great.

Nil Nil

Just as any truly accurate representation of a particular geography can only exist on a scale of 1:1 (imagine the vast, rustling map of Burgundy, say, settling over it like a freshly-starched sheet!) so it is with all our abandoned histories, those ignoble lines of succession that end in neither triumph nor disaster, but merely plunge on into deeper and deeper obscurity; only in the infinite ghost-libraries of the imagination – their only possible analogue – can their ends be pursued, the dull and terrible facts finally authenticated.

François Aussemain, *Pensées*

From the top, then, the zenith, the silent footage:
McGrandle, majestic in ankle-length shorts,
his golden hair shorn to an open book, sprinting
the length of the park for the long hoick forward,
his balletic toe-poke nearly bursting the roof
of the net; a shaky pan to the Erskine St End
where a plague of grey bonnets falls out of the clouds.
But ours is a game of two halves, and this game
the semi they went on to lose; from here
it's all down, from the First to the foot of the Second,
McGrandle, Visocchi and Spankie detaching
like bubbles to speed the descent into pitch-sharing,
pay-cuts, pawned silver, the Highland Division,
the absolute sitters ballooned over open goals,
the dismal nutmegs, the scores so obscene
no respectable journal will print them; though one day
Farquhar's spectacular bicycle-kick
will earn him a name-check in Monday's obituaries.
Besides the one setback — the spell of giant-killing
in the Cup (Lochee Violet, then Aberdeen Bon Accord,
the deadlock with Lochee Harp finally broken
by Farquhar's own-goal in the replay)
nothing inhibits the fifty-year slide
into Sunday League, big tartan flasks,
open hatchbacks parked squint behind goal-nets,
the half-time satsuma, the dog on the pitch,

then the Boy's Club, sponsored by Skelly Assurance,
then Skelly Dry Cleaners, then nobody;
stud-harrowed pitches with one-in-five inclines,
grim fathers and perverts with Old English Sheepdogs
lining the touch, moaning softly.
Now the unrefereed thirty-a-sides,
terrified fat boys with callipers minding
four jackets on infinite, notional fields;
ten years of dwindling, half-hearted kickabouts
leaves two little boys – Alastair Watt,
who answers to 'Forty', and wee Horace Madden,
so smelly the air seems to quiver above him —
playing desperate two-touch with a bald tennis ball
in the hour before lighting-up time.
Alastair cheats, and goes off with the ball
leaving wee Horace to hack up a stone
and dribble it home in the rain;
past the stopped swings, the dead shanty-town
of allotments, the black shell of Skelly Dry Cleaners
and into his cul-de-sac, where, accidentally,
he neatly back-heels it straight into the gutter
then tries to swank off like he meant it.

Unknown to him, it is all that remains
of a lone fighter-pilot, who, returning at dawn
to find Leuchars was not where he'd left it,
took time out to watch the Sidlaws unsheathed
from their great black tarpaulin, the haar burn off Tayport
and Venus melt into Carnoustie, igniting
the shoreline; no wind, not a cloud in the sky
and no one around to admire the discretion
of his unscheduled exit: the engine plopped out
and would not re-engage, sending him silently

twirling away like an ash-key,
his attempt to bail out only partly successful,
yesterday having been April the 1st —
the ripcord unleashing a flurry of socks
like a sackful of doves rendered up to the heavens
in private irenicon. He caught up with the plane
on the ground, just at the instant the tank blew
and made nothing of him, save for his fillings,
his tackets, his lucky half-crown and his gallstone,
now anchored between the steel bars of a stank
that looks to be biting the bullet on this one.

In short, this is where you get off, reader;
I'll continue alone, on foot, in the failing light,
following the trail as it steadily fades
into road-repairs, birdsong, the weather, nirvana,
the plot thinning down to a point so refined
not even the angels could dance on it. Goodbye.

The Queen of Sheba

Scotland, you have invoked her name
just once too often
in your Presbyterian living rooms.
She's heard, yea
even unto heathenish Arabia
your vixen's bark of poverty, come down
the family like a lang neb, a thrawn streak,
a wally dug you never liked
but can't get shot of.

She's had enough. She's come.
Whit, tae this dump? Yes!
She rides first camel
of a swaying caravan
from her desert sands
to the peat and bracken
of the Pentland hills
across the fit-ba pitch
to the thin mirage
of the swings and chute; scattered with glass.

Breathe that steamy musk
on the Curriehill Road, not mutton-shanks
boiled for broth, nor the chlorine stink
of the swimming pool where skinny girls
accuse each other of verrucas.
In her bathhouses women bear
warm pot-bellied terracotta pitchers
on their laughing hips.
All that she desires, whatever she asks
She will make the bottled dreams
of your wee lasses
look like *sweeties.*

Spangles scarcely cover
her gorgeous breasts, hanging gardens
jewels, frankincense; more voluptuous
even than Vi-next-door, whose
high-heeled slippers
keeked from dressing gowns
like little hooves, wee tails
of pink fur stuffed in the cleavage of her toes;
more audacious even than Currie Liz
who led the gala floats
through the Wimpey scheme
in a ruby-red Lotus Elan
before the Boys' Brigade band
and the Brownies' borrowed coal-truck;
hair piled like candy-floss;
who lifted her hands from the neat wheel
to tinkle her fingers
at her tricks
          among the Masons and the elders and the police.

The cool black skin
of the Bible couldn't hold her,
nor the atlas green
on the kitchen table,
you stuck with thumbs
and split to fruity hemispheres -
yellow Yemen, Red Sea, *Ethiopia*. Stick in
with the homework and you'll be
cliver like yer faither.
but no too cliver,
no *above yersel.*

See her lead those great soft camels
widdershins round the kirk-yaird,

smiling
as she eats
avocados with apostle spoons
she'll teach us how. But first

she wants to strip the willow
she desires the keys
        to the National Library
she is beckoning
    the lasses
    in the awestruck crowd...

Yes, we'd like to
        clap the camels,
to smell the spice,
admire her hairy legs and
bonny wicked smile, we want to take
PhDs in Persian, be vice
to her president: we want
to help her
    ask some Difficult Questions

she's shouting for our wisest man
to test her mettle:

    Scour Scotland for a Solomon!

Sure enough: from the back of the crowd
someone growls:
            whae do you think y'ur?

and a thousand laughing girls and she
draw our hot breath
        and shout:

THE QUEEN OF SHEBA!

There are words

for a particular size of stone about the size of your fist
for water only just enough to cover something
for little walks which an invalid could be expected to take

for a rocky hillocky bit of land still capable of cultivation for the most part
for a small triangular piece of land that can be ploughed only on one side
for land from which two crops have been taken in succession

for the left hand side of a furrow
for half of a pair
for the night after tomorrow night

which have been recorded in word lists
compiled on the outer islands with spoken examples
from old persons who still had their wits
in a language not even my grandparents understood;

and shall our descendants some day
be curious to know the words we have,
though I have not found them, giving examples
and idiom of use, explaining the context

for the sort of attention needed driving on a motor-way
for the attention driving slowly on a winding country road
for driving to and from work as you have done perhaps too often

for land approved for development but still standing idle
for land that attracts subsidy provided it stands idle
for land that has been re-zoned and is suddenly valuable

for the time you get for the smallest coin
for the simultaneous programme on the other channel
for a duplicate of a duplicate

for delight in remarking on small details
for the enjoyment of exploring dictionaries
for the indulgence of finding words?

Gael Turnbull | 1995

The King and Queen of Dumfriesshire

The King and Queen of Dumfriesshire sit
in their battery-dead Triumph, gazing ahead
at an iced-over windscreen like a gull rolled flat.
They are cast in bronze, with Henry Moore holes
shot in each other by incessant argument;
these are convenient for holding her tartan flask,
his rolled-up *Scotsman*. The hairy skeleton
of a Border terrier sits in the back window,
not nodding. On the back seat rests
their favourite argument, the one about
how he does not permit her to see the old friends
she no longer likes and he secretly misses;
the one which is really about punishing each other
for no longer wanting to make love.
The argument is in the form of a big white bowl
with a black band around it hand-painted with fruit.
It has a gold rim, and in it lies
a brown curl of water from the leaking roof.
Outside, the clouds continue
to bomb the glen with sheep, which bare
their slate teeth as they tumble,
unexpectedly sneering.
The King and Queen of Dumfriesshire sit
like the too-solid bullet-ridden ghosts
of Bonny and Clyde, not eating their
tinned salmon sandwiches, crustless, still
wrapped in tinfoil, still in the tupperware.
They survey their domain, not glancing at
each other, not removing from the glove compartment
any of the old words they have always used,
words like 'twae', like 'couthy', like 'Kirkcudbright',
which keep their only threat at bay: of separation.

Epithalamium: II, Heimweh

Remembering the story of a man
who left the village one bright afternoon,
wandering out in his shirt-sleeves and never returning,
I walk in this blur of heat to the harbour wall,
and sit with my hands in my pockets, gazing back
at painted houses, shopfronts, narrow roofs,
people about their business, neighbours, tourists,
the gaunt men loading boats with lobster creels,
women in hats and coats, despite the sun,
walking to church and gossip.
It seems too small, too thoroughly contained,
the quiet affliction of home and its meek adjustments,
dogs in the backstreets, barking at every noise,
tidy gardens, crammed with bedding plants.
I turn to the grey of the sea and the further shore:
the thought of distance, endless navigation,
and wonder where he went, that quiet husband,
leaving his keys, his money,
his snow-blind life. It's strange how the ones who vanish
seem weightless and clean, as if they have stepped away
to the near-angelic.
The clock strikes four. On the sea wall, the boys from the village
are stripped to the waist and plunging in random pairs
to the glass-smooth water;
they drop feet first, or curl their small, hard bodies to a ball
and disappear for minutes in the blue.
It's hard not to think this moment is all they desire,
the best ones stay down longest, till their friends
grow anxious, then they re-emerge
like cormorants, some yards from where they dived,
renewing their pact with the air, then swimming back
to start again. It's endlessly repeatable, their private game,
exclusive, pointless, wholly improvised.

John Burnside | 1997

I watch them for a while, then turn for home,
made tentative, half-waiting for the day
I lock my door for good, and leave behind
the smell of fish and grain, your silent fear,
our difficult and unrelenting love.

faclan, eich-mhara

nam bhruadar bha mi nam ghrunnd na mara
agus thu fhèin nad chuan trom
a' leigeil do chudruim orm
agus d' fhaclan gaoil socair nam chluasan
an dràsda 's a-rithist
òrach grinn ainneamh
man eich-mhara, man notaichean-maise
sacsafonaichean beaga fleòdradh

words, seahorses

i dreamt i was the seafloor and you were the weight of ocean pressing
down on me, your quiet words of love in my ears now and again,
golden, elegant and strange, like seahorses, like grace-notes, tiny
floating saxophones

Kevin MacNeil | 1998

from A Nest of Boxes for the Opening of the Scottish Parliament

(...)

First lay its meaning out flat. Then run your finger
over it, from one horizon to the next,
opening and closing, opening and closing it,
as if you were conceding that famous northern threnody
for squeeze-box and bag of guts—

a life-line,
a horse's skull,
a foetus with its thumb in mouth,
a knot,
a Viking long-ship,
a crannog,
a minister's falsers,
a day like any day,
a himberry,
a stone skimmed across water,
a bullet,
an egg-bed,
a rare walnut,
a whorlbane,
a washed-up tyre,
a garnet,
a cutty sark,
a queeny,
a fluky goal,
a dwam,
a poor-box shilling,
a shot star,
a stug of burning bush,
a fit-ba,
a V of migrating geese,

a lily-loch,
a dagger over words of the Older Scottish Tongue,
a grannie's hankie.

(...)

not forgetting how many box-owners, exhausted by time,
walked up their spines to find another box,
one bolted unalterably home though not by themselves—

Linnaeus on Jacob's Ladder,
a spatter of poppies,
soor plooms,
headed notepaper from the John Knox Institute, Geneva,
the Book of Esther,
Sir Mungo Lockhart of the Lea,
Sandy Traill's lament,
things hidden in plain sight,
Engineers Street,
oatmeal with everything,
Pictish Made Easy,
St Kilda's parliament and the eighteen voices answering in chorus,
umbersorrow,
Edwin Muir in the bone factory,
the Old Firm,
forever under the pigeon,
our figurehead coming through the rye,
sheets of rain,
no more shortbread,
a tax on excessive use of the first person plural,
proceedings of the Scotia Bar,
Beuys on Rannoch Moor,
grey zones,
silence (the terrible surrounder),

friends on the Faroes,
Patagonistics,
the undersea Sargossa off the Hebrides,
redcoats landing in France, again,
milk wort and bog-cotton,
my country doctor's box-coat bellying in the wind,
things as guarantors of belonging,
truly remarkable things,
facts unfurling,
quite unremarkable things.

(...)

A Woman Absent from the Museum Muses on her Life in South Dunedin

Those of us whom no one thought to photograph
are here as ghosts   to give the lie
to bread without scarceness   freedom by
honest toil   our lungs choked with the motes
of our sewing, its fibres wound around our throats
and lives: a narrative of nights
without coals to keep the grate alight
of eyes sunk into pouches of skin and sleep
of fingers bound by need to the incessant needle

No new world   No paradise
a grime-smeared house where damp clung
to the weather boards   a valley where smoke hung
all year above a clanking factory
and yet we dreamt   of wonderful simplicities:
fresh vegetables in a cottage garden
a geranium on a window sill   and everything clean
We dreamt   for dreaming's free, nothing
could stop us   of what we had been promised
of what bread without scarceness might have meant

Gerrie Fellows | 2000

Orkney / This Life

for Catherine & Jamie

It is big sky and its changes,
the sea all round and the waters within.
It is the way sea and sky
work off each other constantly,
like people meeting in Alfred Street,
each face coming away with a hint
of the other's face pressed in it.
It is the way a week-long gale
ends, and folk emerge to hear
a single bird cry way high up.

It is the way you lean to me
and the way I lean to you, as if
we are each other's prevailing;
how we connect along our shores,
the way we are tidal islands
joined for hours then inaccessible –
I'll go for that, and smile when I
pick sand off myself in the shower.
The way I am an inland loch to you
when a clatter of white whoops and rises...

It is the way Scotland looks to the South,
the way we enter friends' houses
to leave what we came with, or flick
the kettle's switch and wait.
This is where I want to live,
close to where the heart gives out,
ruined, perfected, an empty arch against the sky
where birds fly through instead of prayers
while in Hoy Sound the ferry's engines thrum
this life this life this life.

The world is busy, Katie

The world is busy, Katie, and tonight
the planes are playing, fine, alright, but soon
the folk behind those blinks will nap, sleep tight
as you will too, beneath a nitelite moon.
The world is busy, Katie, but it's late –
the trains are packing up, the drunks are calm.
The fast, the slow, has gone. It's only freight
that storms the garage lane. It means no harm.
The world is busy, Katie, but it's dark –
the lorries nod, they snort, they spoil their chrome.
They hate to be alone. They look to park
just off the road. For them, a lay-by's home.
The world is busy, Katie, like I said,
but you're the world – and tired. It's time for bed.

Richard Price | 2002

Poets' Biographies
with sources for the poems

IAIN BAMFORTH, 1959–

Iain Bamforth was born in 1959 into a Plymouth Brethren family and grew up in Glasgow, where he attended the university. He ran his own medical practice in Strasbourg, and currently teaches modern German literature in translation at Strasbourg University. He contributes regularly to a number of periodicals including *PN Review*, *Times Literary Supplement* and *New York Times Book Review*. He edited *The Body in the Library: A Literary Anthology of Modern Medicine* (2003).

'A Nest of Boxes for the Opening of the Scottish Parliament', in *The Scotsman*, 2 July 1999. Also published in *Without Day: proposals for a new Scottish Parliament*, edited by Alec Finlay (Edinburgh: pocketbooks, 2000).

See also: *Open Workings* (Manchester: Carcanet, 1996).

MEG BATEMAN, 1959–

Meg Bateman was born and brought up in Edinburgh. She learnt Gaelic as an adult in South Uist and at Aberdeen University. She works at Sabhal Mòr Ostaig – Scotland's only Gaelic college – on the Isle of Skye, where she lives with her son. As well as poems, she has also published translations of older Gaelic poetry, and scholarly articles.

'Aotramachd', in *Verse*, vol. 6, no. 3 (Winter 1989); p.42. Also published in *Aotromachd agus dain eile/Lightness and other poems* (Edinburgh: Polygon, 1997).

JOHN BURNSIDE, 1955–

John Burnside has published eight collections of poetry, most recently *The Light Trap* (2002). His seventh collection, *The Asylum Dance*, won the 2000 Whitbread Poetry Award, and was shortlisted for both the Forward and T.S. Eliot Prize. He has also published five works of fiction, including, most recently, *Living Nowhere*. He lives in Fife, and is a lecturer in Creative Writing at the University of St Andrews.

'Epithalamium: II, Heimweh', in *A Normal Skin* (London: Jonathan Cape, 1997).

ROBERT CRAWFORD, 1959–

Born in Bellshill, he was schooled in Glasgow, then at universities in Glasgow and Oxford. He writes in English and in Scots, and has published five collections of poems. He is Professor of Modern Scottish Literature and Head of the School of English at the University of St Andrews, where he has taught since 1989. With Simon Armitage he edited *The Penguin Book of Poetry from Britain and Ireland since 1945* (1998) and with Mick Imlah *The New Penguin Book of Scottish Verse* (2000).

'Scotland', in *A Scottish Assembly* (London : Chatto & Windus, 1990).

See also: *Spirit Machines* (London : Cape Poetry, 1999); and *The Tip of my Tongue* (London : Cape, 2003).

CAROL ANN DUFFY, 1955–

Born in Glasgow, Carol Ann Duffy moved with her family to Stafford when she was five. After studying at Liverpool University, she lived in London from 1981 to 1995; since 1996 she has lived in Manchester. A popular poet whose work is widely studied in secondary schools, she has also published collections of poems for children. She teaches at Manchester Metropolitan University.

'Warming her Pearls', in *Selling Manhattan* (London : Anvil Press Poetry, 1987). Also published in *Selected Poems* (London : Penguin, 1994).

DOUGLAS DUNN, 1942–

Douglas Dunn was born in Renfrewshire in 1942. After working as a librarian in Scotland and Akron, Ohio, he studied English at Hull University. He then worked for eighteen months in the university library after which, in 1971, he became a freelance writer. In 1991 he was appointed Professor in the School of English at the University of St Andrews. As well as ten collections of poetry, Dunn has written several radio and television plays, and edited *The Faber Book of Twentieth-Century Scottish Poetry* (1992).

'Empires', in *Barbarians* (London : Faber, 1979). Also published in *New Selected Poems : 1964–2000* (London : Faber, 2003).

GERRIE FELLOWS, 1954–

Gerrie Fellows was born in New Zealand of Scottish descent, her family moving to England in 1963. She has lived in Glasgow for nearly twenty years and works as a creative writing tutor. *The Powerlines* traces Scottish and New Zealand connections through a variety of women's voices. Her latest collection, *The Duntroon Toponymy*, was published by Mariscat in 2001.

'A Woman Absent from the Museum Muses on her Life in South Dunedin', in *The Powerlines* (Edinburgh : Polygon, 2000).

ROBIN FULTON, 1937–

Robin Fulton was born on the island of Arran. He spent his childhood there, in the Glasgow area, and in Sutherland. After studying at Edinburgh University, he became a schoolteacher. Since 1973 he has lived in Stavanger, Norway, where he works as a university lecturer. Between 1967 and 1976 he edited the Scottish literary magazine *Lines Review*; he also edited Iain Crichton Smith's *Selected Poems* (1981) and Robert Garioch's *Complete Poetical Works* (1983). He is well known as a translator of Swedish, Norwegian and Danish poetry.

'Museums and Journeys', in *Fields of Focus* (London : Anvil P., 1982).

See also: *Coming down to earth and Spring is soon* (London/Plymouth : Oasis/ Shearsman, 1990).

ANDREW GREIG, 1951–

Andrew Greig was born in Bannockburn, and studied Philosophy at the University of Edinburgh. *Summit Fever* (1985) and *Kingdoms of Experience* (1986) chronicle his participation in major climbing expeditions. His six books of poetry range from short love lyrics to the epic *Men on Ice* (1977), an ironic play on the Grail quest. He has also written several novels, including *When They Lay Bare* (1999), based on the Border ballad 'The Twa Corbies'. He lives in Orkney and the Lothians.

'Orkney/This Life', in *Into You* (Tarset : Bloodaxe, 2001).

GEORGE CAMPBELL HAY, 1915–1984

Hay grew up in Kintyre, before attending school in Edinburgh, and university in Oxford. During the war he spent time in North Africa and Italy, before being transferred to Greece, where a violent incident led to the onset of a mental illness which was to dog him for the rest of his life. A prolific linguist and translator, his poems are principally in Gaelic, but he also wrote in Scots, English, Italian, French, Danish and other languages.

'She's a solan...', in *Seeker, Reaper* (Edinburgh : Saltire Society, 1988). Also published in *Collected Poems and Songs of George Campbell Hay*, edited by Michel Byrne (Edinburgh : Edinburgh U.P. for Lorimer Trust, 2000).

www.eup.ed.ac.uk/NewWeb/GCH1.htm

W.N. HERBERT, 1961–

Born in Dundee, he was educated there and at Brasenose College, Oxford. He mainly writes poetry in Scots and English, but a number of essays and short stories have also been published. He reviews for, among others, the newspaper *Scotland on Sunday*. He has held Writer in Residence posts in Dumfries & Galloway, and in Moray. From 1996 to 2002 he taught at Lancaster University. He now lectures in Creative Writing and Contemporary Scottish Poetry at the University of Newcastle upon Tyne.

'The King and Queen of Dumfriesshire', in *Cabaret McGonagall* (Newcastle upon Tyne: Bloodaxe, 1996).

www.xen19.dial.pipex.com

KATHLEEN JAMIE, 1962–

Kathleen Jamie was born in the west of Scotland, and educated in Edinburgh, where she studied Philosophy. *Mr & Mrs Scotland are Dead* was shortlisted for the International Griffin Poetry Prize, and in 2002 she was awarded a Creative Scotland Award. As well as poetry Kathleen Jamie writes non-fiction. She holds a part-time post as Lecturer in Creative Writing at St Andrews University and lives in Fife.

'The Queen of Sheba', in *The Queen of Sheba* (Newcastle upon Tyne: Bloodaxe, 1994). Also published in *Mr and Mrs Scotland are Dead: Poems 1980–1994 by Kathleen Jamie*, selected by Lilias Fraser (Tarset: Bloodaxe, 2002).

TOM LEONARD, 1944–

Born in Glasgow, Tom Leonard is best known for poetry written in the urban speech of that city. This, and his seminal critical writings, have had a major impact on attitudes to language in Scotland, and beyond. He also edited the ground-breaking anthology *Radical Renfrew*, and wrote a biography of the 19th century poet James Thomson, *Places of the Mind*. In 2002, jointly with Alasdair Gray and James Kelman, he was appointed Professor of Creative Writing at Glasgow Univeristy.

'right inuff', in *Ghostie Men* (Newcastle upon Tyne: Galloping Dog P., 1980). Also published in *Intimate Voices* (Buckfastleigh: Etruscan, 2003).

See also: *access to the silence: Poems 1984–2004* (Buckfastleigh: Etruscan, 2004).

www.tomleonard.co.uk

LIZ LOCHHEAD, 1947–

Born in Motherwell, and trained at Glasgow School of Art, in 1972 Liz Lochhead published her first collection, *Memo for Spring*, with immediate success. In the predominantly male domain of Scottish poetry, hers was a fresh voice, of women speaking to women, speaking for women. Her poems, prose and drama escape the boundaries of each genre, using the speech she hears around her, poignant and humorous, to question assumptions about female and Scottish identity.

'My Rival's House', in *The Grimm Sisters* (London: Next Editions/Faber, 1981). Also published in *Dreaming Frankenstein: and collected poems 1967–1984* (Edinburgh: Polygon, 2003).

See also: *The Colour of Black and White: Poems 1984–2003* (Edinburgh: Polygon, 2003).

Norman MacCaig, 1910–1996

Norman MacCaig was born in Edinburgh, of a lowland father and a highland mother. At the University of Edinburgh he studied Classics, before working for many years as a primary school teacher. A conscientious objector during the Second World War, his first two books were published in the 1940s, though he later disowned them. From *Riding Lights* in 1955 to *Voice Over* in 1988 he published fourteen collections of poetry. For most of his life, MacCaig divided his time between Edinburgh and Assynt in the north-west highlands: the Assynt landscape is a recurring theme of his poetry.

'By the graveyard, Luskentyre', in *Collected Poems* (London: Chatto & Windus/Hogarth P., 1985).

www.jacobite.org.uk/maccaig/
www.spl.org.uk/poets_pub/maccaig_com.html

Aonghas Macneacail, 1942–

Aonghas Macneacail was born in Uig on Skye. He is a poet, journalist, researcher, broadcaster, scriptwriter and filmmaker. He has published collections of poems in both Gaelic and English and his writing has appeared in literary journals in Scotland and internationally. He has had poetry broadcast on radio, television, has given readings throughout Scotland and has toured extensively abroad. He won the Stakis Prize for Scottish Writer of the Year with his third collection, *Oideachadh Ceart / A proper schooling* in 1997.

'beul beag' in An Aghaidh na Sìorraidheachd: ochdnar bhard Gaidhlig: duanaire dà-chànanach / In the Face of Eternity: eight Gaelic poets: a bilingual anthology, edited by Christopher Whyte (Edinburgh: Polygon, 1991). Also published in *Oideachadh ceart, agus dain eile / A proper schooling, and other poems* (Edinburgh: Polygon, 1996).

www.smo.uhi.ac.uk/~aonghasd/cv.html

Kevin MacNeil, 1972–

Kevin MacNeil was born and raised on the Isle of Lewis. From 1999-2002 he worked as the Writer in Residence for Highland Council. During this time he edited two collections of short stories by Iain Crichton Smith. In 2002 he moved to Sweden for a year to be the British Council Writer in Residence at Uppsala University. He is currently again living on Lewis.

'faclan, eich-mhara', in *Love and Zen in the Outer Hebrides* (Edinburgh: Canongate, 1998).

www.angelfire.com/poetry/loveandzen/index.html

Edwin Morgan, 1920–

Born Glasgow, 1920, Edwin Morgan has lived in Glasgow all his life, except for service with the RAMC in the Middle East during the Second World War. His poetry is grounded in the city, though he is also a prolific translator from many languages. He retired from Glasgow University as titular Professor of English in 1980, serving as Glasgow's first Poet Laureate 1999-2002. In February 2004 he became the first 'Scots Makar', in effect Scotland's poet laureate.

'The Coin', in *Glasgow Magazine, no. 1* (Winter 1982/83). Also published in *Collected Poems* (Manchester: Carcanet, 1990).

See also: *Collected Translations* (Manchester: Carcanet, 1996).

www.edwinmorgan.com

www.spl.org.uk/poets_pub/morgan_com.html

Don Paterson, 1963–

Born in Dundee in 1963, Don Paterson left school to pursue a career in music, living in London and Brighton. He returned to Dundee in 1993 as Writer in Residence at the University, and at the end of his tenure went to London to take up the position of poetry editor at Picador in 1995, a position he still holds. He now lives with his family in Kirriemuir, continuing to work as a musician, editor and writer.

'Nil Nil', in *Nil Nil* (London: Faber, 1993).

www.donpaterson.com

Richard Price, 1965–

Richard Price was born in Reading in 1966 and grew up in Renfrewshire. He was educated at Napier College and the University of Strathclyde, and now works as curator of Modern British Collections at the British Library. He is co-founder of the Vennel Press, a London publisher with a Scottish accent. He has published several collections of poems, and a book of short stories, *A Boy in Summer* (2002).

'The world is busy, Katie', in *Frosted, Melted* (Callander: diehard, 2002).

Seán Rafferty, 1909–1993

Seán Rafferty was born in Dumfriesshire. He read English Literature under Herbert Grierson at Edinburgh University, where he knew Sorley MacLean. He went to London, and for a time he worked at the Players Theatre. He became a publican in Devon. During his lifetime he published little, but agreed shortly before his death to a *Collected Poems*.

'Peacocks', in *Peacocks was really great* [1992: bibliographical details unavailable]. Also published in *Poems by Seán Rafferty*, edited by Nicholas Johnson (Buckfastleigh: Etruscan, 1999).

Alastair Reid, 1926–

Alastair Reid was born in 1926 in Galloway, and graduated from the University of St Andrews after war service in the navy. He has lived in Spain, France, Switzerland, the United States, and Central and South America, writing for many years for *The New Yorker*. As a translator, he is best known for his English versions of work by Neruda and Borges, both of whom he knew.

'My Father, Dying', in *Weathering: poems and translations* (Edinburgh: Canongate, 1978).

See also: *Oases: poems and prose* (Edinburgh : Canongate, 1997).

Iain Crichton Smith, 1928–1998

Brought up on the island of Lewis, Iain Crichton Smith spent most of his working life as a schoolteacher, in Clydebank then Oban. He wrote prose and poetry in both Gaelic and English. Often a deeply troubled man, and a self-deprecating writer, he could move an audience to tears of laughter with his 'Murdo' stories. *Consider the Lilies*, about the Highland Clearances, is a classic novel, but he considered himself more naturally a poet.

'Iolaire', in *The Exiles* (Manchester/Dublin : Carcanet P./Raven Arts P., 1984). Also published in *Collected Poems* (Manchester : Carcanet, 1992).

www.arts.gla.ac.uk/ScotLit/ASLS/ICSmith.html

www.spl.org.uk/poets_pub/crichton_com.html

Alan Spence, 1947–

Alan Spence, author of poetry, novels, short stories and plays, was born in Glasgow. As a poet, Alan Spence uses the haiku form to explore the essential paradox of life, discovering timelessness in cycles of changes, and simplicity in the intricate. He has received many awards for his writing. Alan Spence splits his time between Edinburgh, where he and his wife run the Chinmoy Meditation Centre, and Aberdeen, where he is Writer in Residence at the University.

'Five Haiku', in *Alan Spence* (Glasgow: National Book League, 1986). Also published in *Seasons of the heart: haiku* (Edinburgh: Canongate, 2000).

See also: *Glasgow Zen* (Edinburgh : Canongate, 2002).

Gael Turnbull, 1928–2004

Gael Turnbull was born in 1928 in Edinburgh. He spent his working life as a doctor in Canada, the United States, and England, returning to Edinburgh when he retired in 1989. His Migrant Press, founded in 1957 while he was living in California, introduced writers such as Robert Creeley to a British readership, and Ian Hamilton Finlay to an American readership. His poetry is characterized by an unusually wide range of technical resource and invention, extending to his recent kinetic poems, seen on the streets of Edinburgh during the International Festival.

'There are words', in *For Whose Delight* (Glasgow : Mariscat, 1995).

See also: *Time is a Fisherman: Selected Poems* (Buckfastleigh/Glasgow: Etruscan/Mariscat, forthcoming in spring 2005).

Further details of the following poets can be found at the British Council website www.contemporarywriters.com

John Burnside
Robert Crawford
Carol Ann Duffy
Douglas Dunn
Andrew Greig
W.N. Herbert
Kathleen Jamie
Liz Lochhead
Don Paterson

The Editors

Ken Cockburn is Assistant Director at the Scottish Poetry Library, where he has worked since 1996. For the SPL he edited, with Alec Finlay, the audio-CD *The Jewel Box: Contemporary Scottish Poems*. He was also Project Director for pocketbooks, for whom he edited *The Order of Things: Scottish sound, pattern and concrete poems*. His own poems are published in *Souvenirs and Homelands*, and more recently in various anthologies including *Dream State*. He lives in Edinburgh.

New Zealand-born Robyn Marsack has been Director of the Scottish Poetry Library since 2000. After moving to Scotland in 1987, she worked as a freelance editor, critic and translator, and has had a long editorial association with Carcanet Press. Her published work includes studies of Louis MacNeice and Sylvia Plath. She lives in Glasgow.

Acknowledgements

Our thanks are due to the following authors, publishers, and estates who have generously given permission to reproduce works.

The poems by Iain Bamforth, Robin Fulton, Tom Leonard, Richard Price, Alastair Reid and Alan Spence are reprinted by permission of the authors.

The poem by Seán Rafferty is reprinted by permission of the Estate of Seán Rafferty.

The poem by Carol Ann Duffy is reprinted by permission of Anvil Press Poetry; those by Kathleen Jamie, W. N. Herbert and Andrew Greig, reprinted by permission of Bloodaxe Books; those by Liz Lochhead, Meg Bateman, Aonghas MacNeacail and Gerrie Fellows, reprinted by permission of Birlinn; that by Kevin MacNeil, reprinted by permission of Canongate Books; those by Edwin Morgan and Iain Crichton Smith, reprinted by permission of Carcanet Press; that by George Campbell Hay, reprinted by permission of Edinburgh University Press; those by Douglas Dunn and Don Paterson, reprinted by permission of Faber and Faber; that by Gael Turnbull, reprinted by permission of Mariscat Press.

The poems by Norman MacCaig (from *Collected Poems* by Norman MacCaig, published by Chatto & Windus), Robert Crawford (from *A Scottish Assembly* by Robert Crawford, published by Chatto & Windus), and John Burnside (from *A Normal Skin* by John Burnside, published by Jonathan Cape) are all reprinted by permission of The Random House Group Ltd.

Every effort has been made to trace copyright holders of the poems published in this book. The editors and publishers apologise if any material has been included without the appropriate acknowledgement, and would be glad to correct any oversights in future editions.

Forthcoming titles in the series XXV

Hungarian Original: XXV Hungarian Poems 1978-2002

Edited by István Turczi and with an Introduction by Béla Pomogáts

István Turczi, with his wife Anna Palos Turczi, runs the publishing house Parnasszus, producing a quarterly literary magazine of the same name, as well as books by contemporary Hungarian poets, translators and essayists. He is also a poet, novelist, dramatist and translator. The poets included are István Baka, Zsófia Balla, Lászlo Benjamin, Gyõzõ Csorba, György Faludy, Gyõzõ Ferencz, Ágnes Gergely, Gyula Illyés, László Kálnoky, István Kemény, Endre Kukorelly, Lászlo Lator, Ágnes Nemes Nagy, Ottó Orbán, György Petri, Sándor Rákos, Zsuzsa Rakovszky, Zsuzsa Takács, Dezsõ Tandori, János Térey, Krisztina Tóth, István Turczi, Szabolcs Várady, István Vas, Sándor Weöres. The poems have been translated into Scots and English by Ron Butlin, Tom Hubbard, Edwin Morgan, Angus Reid and Christopher Whyte. Zsuzsa Varga has acted as language advisor for the anthology.

ISBN 1 85754 796 9, March 2005, £7.95

Finnish Original: XXV Finnish poems 1978-2002

Edited and with an Introduction by Anni Sumari

Sumari's choice includes work by Finnish modernists such as Paavo Haavikko and Lassi Nummi; several prose poems, the prevalence of which in recent Finnish literature she discusses in her Introduction; and aphoristic poems. 22 of her selections were written in Finnish, with 3 examples of writing in Finland-Swedish. Anni Sumari has published nine books of short stories and poetry, as well as a travelogue about a writers' train that toured Europe in 2000. Her poems have been translated into many languages, including Russian, German and Spanish. She has rendered into Finnish a collection of Samuel Beckett's short stories. The poets included are Gösta Ågren, Kari Aronpuro, Bo Carpelan, Tua Forsström, Paavo Haavikko, Anne Hänninen, Hannu Helin, Markku Into, Eeva Kilpi, Eila Kivikk'aho, Juhani Koskinen, Jarkko Laine, Rakel Liehu, Arto Melleri, Lassi Nummi, Lauri Otonkoski, Markku Paasonen, Mirkka Rekola, Pentti Saarikoski, Helena Sinervo, Eira Stenberg, Anni Sumari, Arja Tiainen, Sirkka Turkka.

ISBN 1 85754 816 7, March 2005, £7.95